THE GREAT ARTISTS
& THEIR WORLD
PICASSO

NEW
FOREST
PRESS

Publisher: Melissa Fairley
Editor: Guy Croton
Designer: Carol Davis
Production Controller: Ed Green
Production Manager: Suzy Kelly

ISBN: 978-1-84898-314-4
Library of Congress Control Number: 2010925217
Tracking number: nfp0004

North American edition copyright © TickTock Entertainment Ltd. 2010
First published in North America in 2010 by New Forest Press,
PO Box 784, Mankato, MN 56002
www.newforestpress.com

Printed in the USA
9 8 7 6 5 4 3 2 1

CONTENTS

INTRODUCTION

Pablo Picasso is one of the most influential artists of the twentieth century. Usually known simply by one name (even though he actually had 14) he is famous for starting and shaping several different styles and art movements and over the course of his 91 years, for changing modern art completely.

CHILD PRODIGY

Born in southern Spain at the end of the nineteenth century, Picasso showed his artistic genius from an early age. As a teenager, he painted in a realistic and technically accomplished style and he grew up to experiment with many different techniques, theories, and ideas. His revolutionary achievements brought him widespread recognition and prosperity, making him arguably the most famous artist of his time. During his seventy-five year career, he worked as a painter, draughtsman, printer, sculptor, and ceramicist and produced over 20,000 works. Bold, versatile, and diverse, he is probably best known for co-founding the Cubist movement with fellow artist Georges Braque and for painting groundbreaking works such as *Les Demoiselles d'Avignon* and *Guernica.*

INSPIRATION

The son of a painter, curator, and art teacher, Picasso's inventiveness began at an early age. By the age of thirteen he was accepted at the School of Fine Arts in Barcelona, where he completed the entrance exam in a day that took older students over a month. Five years later, he moved to Paris. When his friend Casagemas committed suicide, Picasso began painting sad-looking, elongated subjects inspired by the sixteenth century artist El Greco, in shades of blue. This later became called his Blue Period. Three years later, he began painting in warmer colors, mainly in pinks and beiges. This became known as his Rose Period. From 1905, after a visit to Holland and meeting Matisse in Paris, he started experimenting with media and styles. That year he visited an exhibition of paintings in bright and discordant colors by Matisse and some likeminded friends in Paris. The artists were nicknamed "Les Fauves," which is French for "wild beasts." This and the work of the self-taught "naïve" French painter Henri Rousseau gave him more ideas. He found inspiration everywhere—from Iberian sculptures at the Louvre to children's toys and drawings, from the Impressionists' focus on light to African masks—nothing was left unexplored once it caught his eye. But his main stimulation came from Cézanne's work and theories about painting. He began exploring ways of representing three dimensions on two dimensional surfaces and in 1907, produced *Les Demoiselles d'Avignon*, a work that changed everything that had been valued in painting until then. Although shocking at first, it was soon considered one of the most significant paintings of the twentieth century and it led to the development of Cubism.

CUBISM AND AFTER

For some years, Picasso and Braque worked together, producing images that showed several angles of the subjects they were painting at once. The idea was that photographs can snap images from one angle, but paintings can do more, by showing a subject from numerous views simultaneously. Until 1912 they painted in subdued colors with geometric forms. This became called Analytical Cubism. Next, their work featured more decorative shapes, stenciling, collage, and slightly brighter colors and became known as Synthetic Cubism. By showing objects from different viewpoints, Picasso and Braque challenged the

principles of perspective that had been practiced since the Renaissance. Because their objects appeared splintered and angular, a critic described them as "little cubes"—which became Cubism.

Picasso continued with his artistic inventions. He designed costumes and scenery for the ballet *Parade* in Rome. He became involved in the Surrealist movement and briefly revived neoclassicism. As well as paintings, he experimented with collages, etchings, sculpture, and ceramics. In 1937, during the Spanish Civil War, the Republican government asked him to paint something for the Spanish Pavilion at the Paris Exposition Universelle. They wanted him to glorify Spain, but instead, he painted a huge work showing the effects of the bombing of Guernica, a Spanish town. Painted in black, gray, and white, the monumental painting's distorted images show the horrors of war on innocent people. For the rest of his life, Picasso continued experimenting with styles and materials, never becoming complacent and giving fresh vitality to everything he produced.

Le formule misteriose del "mago": Alberto Einstein, creatore della teoria della relatività che ha aperto la via all'utilizzazione dell'energia atomica, ha enunciato nei giorni scorsi, in una lezione tenuta a Princeton, una nuova geniale teoria sulla concezione dell'universo (vedi altre notizie a pag. 6).

IT'S ALL RELATIVE

In 1905, the German-born scientist Albert Einstein published his first theory of relativity. His theories showed that time would slow down if you could travel at the speed of light, which was the fastest thing in the universe. His discoveries guided nuclear science and the eventual creation of the atomic bomb.

THE WORLD IN THE 1900S

The 19th century is said to have ended not in 1900, but in 1914 with the start of World War I. The period leading up to 1914 was the quiet before the storm, that was to break with such force and devastate a whole generation. Rumblings could be heard in those quiet years which were a prologue to an entirely new era that swept away the old ruling classes in Europe, and changed established ways of thinking forever. It was not just political and social change. Einstein's theories challenged the very principles upon which our knowledge of the world was based. The invention of powered flight, the cinema, wireless communications (radio), and much more was to have an effect far beyond the grasp of those living in the first decade of the 20th century. In 1907, Pablo Picasso painted a picture which broke all the rules of the last 500 years of art. The painting, called *Les Demoiselles d'Avignon* (see pages 20–21), was to have an effect as powerful as any of the inventions of his day.

A CAR FOR EVERYONE

In 1908, Henry Ford opened a factory to produce cars. He used a new method called the "production line" which enabled cars to be manufactured at prices cheap enough for ordinary people to afford.

THE ART CAPITAL

By 1900, Paris had a reputation as the art capital of the world. Artists of all nations traveled to the city to follow in the traditions of the now famous Impressionists such as Claude Monet. They crowded into the bohemian quarter of Montmartre and could be seen in animated discussion in the many cafés which offered cheap food and entertainment.

107. PARIS – Le Métropolitain au Boulevard de la Chapelle   E. L. D.

THE MOVIES

In 1895, the first motion pictures had been presented by the Lumière brothers to a disbelieving audience in Paris. In 1905, a film theater opened in the United States. It charged one nickel admission, and was therefore called the Nickelodeon. In 1907, the motion picture industry found its natural home in the balmy climate of Southern California, and has stayed there ever since.

POWERED FLIGHT

On December 17, 1903 at Kitty Hawk, North Carolina, in the United States, two brothers made the first ever powered flight. The first flight lasted just 12 seconds but subsequent flights lasted up to 59 seconds. Orville and Wilbur Wright, flying in the aircraft they named *Flyer*, ushered in the age of the airplane.

BRITISH IMPERIAL POWER

Victoria, Queen of Great Britain and Ireland, and Empress of India, died in the 64th year of her reign in January, 1901. Victoria had ruled over an empire which touched every corner of the globe and which without doubt exerted the greatest power and influence in the world. The supremacy of the British Naval fleet helped maintain the huge empire which gave Britain enormous wealth. Spurred by commercial competition, rival nations such as Germany began to challenge the dominance of the British Empire.

THE WORLD OF PICASSO

Picasso was born in the Andalusian city of Malaga on the southern coast of Spain on October 25, 1881. Legend has it that at birth he had to be brought to life by an uncle who blew cigar smoke in his nose. When baptized his full name was made up from no fewer than 14 names, the first Pablo, the last two Ruiz Picasso. He eventually came to use his mother's surname, Picasso, in favor of that of his father, Don José Ruiz. His father was a drawing teacher at a local art school who supplemented his poorly paid job with another as curator at the local museum and yet a third as a picture restorer. When Picasso was 10 years old, the local museum closed and Don José took 0a teaching post at the School of Fine Arts in the Atlantic port of Coruna. The family moved with him.

It was shortly afterward that Don José, recognizing his son's talent for art, decided to give up painting himself and concentrate on developing young Pablo Picasso's career as an artist.

THE YOUNG PICASSO

Picasso arrived in Paris in October, 1900, with his companion Carlos Casagemas. They took up residence in the Montmartre studio of a Spanish artist, Isidre Nonell, who had decided to return to Spain. Picasso stayed long enough to find an art dealer who offered to sell his work before returning to spend Christmas with his family in Spain. He went back to Paris in May the following year but his friend Casagemas was dead, having committed suicide after an unhappy love affair.

GIRL WITH BARE FEET, 1895

Picasso was born an artist. It is said that he could draw before he could talk, and when he could talk his first word was "pencil." Don José started teaching his son painting from the age of seven. When he was 13 Picasso finished a sketch his father had started, and when Don José saw what Picasso had done he handed him his palette and brushes, vowing never to paint again. The 13 year old Picasso enrolled at the Academy of Fine Arts where his father taught. When he was 14 he painted *Girl with Bare Feet.* The model is unknown but is clearly of a girl of about the young Picasso'sage. It is a stunning painting for one so young. The picture remained one of Picasso's favorites for many years and may have reminded him of his little sister, Concepcion, who died the same year.

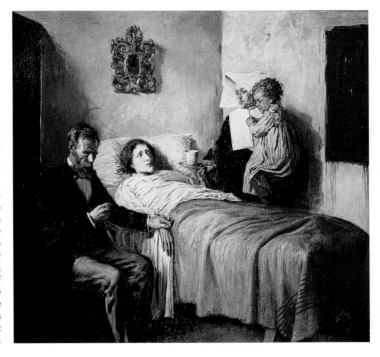

SCIENCE & CHARITY, 1897

Picasso painted this academy piece when he was 15. It received an honorable mention at the National Beaux-Arts exhibition of 1897 and a gold medal in a local competition in Picasso's home town of Malaga. The doctor who is taking the pulse of the sick woman is based on his father, identifiable from the reddish blonde hair. The picture demonstrates Picasso's early artistic skill. Although seeming rather stilted in contrast to *Girl with Bare Feet* it is full of poignancy. Has Picasso reversed the roles of the sick mother and the little daughter who looks on from the nurse's arms? Concepcion's death could not have been far from his thoughts.

LE MOULIN DE LA GALETTE, 1900

Picasso briefly attended the Academy at Madrid, then Barcelona, but his teachers appeared to have nothing to offer him. The city of Barcelona, however, gave Picasso access to new artist friends who copied the bohemian café life of Paris. Picasso gained a sense of freedom, but still wanted to see for himself the new art of London and Paris. In 1900 he set out for London, stopping in Paris on the way. It is no coincidence that his first picture of Paris was of the Moulin de la Galette, a favorite haunt of the Impressionists, who Picasso must have heard so much about.

MUSIC

Henri Mattisse

Matisse, senior to Picasso by 12 years, was working in Paris at the same time as Picasso in the early 1900s. Matisse's obsession was the exploration of color to express emotion. He was the "king" of the Fauvist painters, and was the undisputed leader of the new art, after his exhibition at the Salon in 1906. Picasso, however, was to become more influential, particularly as Cubism with Picasso's involvement became the accepted way forward toward the modern art of the 20th century.

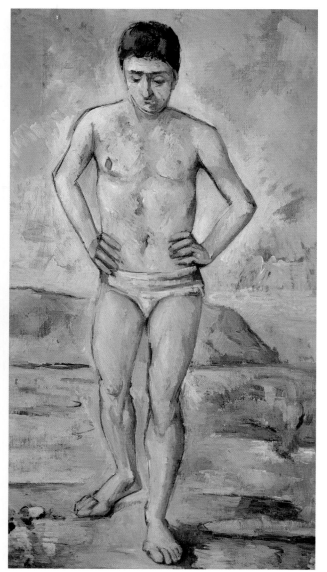

THE GREAT BATHERS

Paul Cézanne

Cézanne was born in the South of France in 1839, only taking up painting when he came to Paris in the 1860s. Although working and exhibiting alongside the Impressionists he was dissatisfied with their approach and said that he wanted to: *"make of Impressionism something solid and durable, like the art of the Museums."* Cézanne's influence on 20th-century art has been profound, many attributing the basic ideas of Cubism— seeking to represent the structure and form of objects not just their surface—to him.

MOULIN ROUGE

Henri Toulouse-Lautrec

Although Lautrec died shortly after Picasso first came to Paris, his work impressed and influenced Picasso. Lautrec's studies of the dance halls and bordellos with their dispassionate gaze onto the seedier side of Parisian life encouraged Picasso to seek similar subjects. Although hints of Lautrec's painterly style can be seen in Picasso's very early paintings from this period, attention to the same subject matter is more noticeable. Picasso's early "Blue Period" paintings, so called because of the predominantly blue hues, include studies of the sick prostitutes who visited the Saint-Lazare hospital.

THE ART OF HIS DAY

Picasso's life and career spanned nearly a century. When he first visited Paris in 1900, he entered a city which was alive with artists pursuing new and different approaches to painting. Impressionism was well known; its leading exponent, Claude Monet, had gained international recognition. Breakaway groups such as the Pointillists were challenging Impressionism; Degas and Renoir were following individual paths; loners such as Gauguin and van Gogh had developed highly individual styles. At first Picasso experimented with these new influences but quickly established his own way of painting, which soon had its followers, known as "La Bande Picasso." By 1905, a new style of painting had developed called Fauvism, led by Henri Matisse (the principle aim of Fauvism was to use color as a means of expression). Matisse and fellow artist Paul Cézanne greatly influenced the course of painting at the beginning of the century, but none has contributed as much as Picasso who always remained an individual while working alongside artistic movements such as Cubism, Surrealism, Expressionism, Futurism, and many more "isms."

LES ACROBATS

Fernand Léger

Léger was one of the painters fully committed to Cubism, along with Braque and Gris, but developed his own particular style which was based on cylindrical and conical forms. Although Picasso painted in a similar way to the Cubist painters from as early as 1909, he was always exploring new methods and styles. When Picasso saw the Cubist paintings in Paris at the Salon des Indepéndants in 1911, he was described by his friend Apollinaire as: *"sympathetic but trying not to laugh."* This is a good example of how Picasso would take what he needed from a new movement in art and then move on, rather than become fixed with one idea and style, as did many of the Cubists.

FAMILY & FRIENDS

PICASSO AND FERNANDE OLIVIER

This photograph, taken in the Café El Guayaba in Barcelona in 1906, shows Picasso with his lover Fernande on his right. Fernande had moved into the Bateau Lavoir with sculptor Debienne. Another affair with painter Sunyer followed, before she moved in with Picasso in 1904. Fernande published her memoirs in 1988, in which she writes about the beginning of her affair with Picasso. *"One Sunday, under a burning sun, I took my things over to Picasso's. A whim had thrown me into your arms one stormy day. Then, suddenly, I withdrew and you suffered from that for months. Then I called you. You were working, but you dropped your canvas and brushes and came running."* It may be that the change from Picasso's melancholy "Blue Period" paintings after the death of friend Casagemas, to the warmer "Rose Period" from 1904 was as a result of his encounter with Fernande.

Picasso resembled his mother, María Picasso López, a petite Andalusian with eyes as black as her hair, rather than his father who was tall with reddish hair which led to his nickname "the Englishman." Picasso was encouraged to draw and paint at an early age by his father, whose own paintings Picasso later described as: *"dining room pictures, the kind with partridges and pigeons, hares and rabbits, fur and feather."* He had two younger sisters, Lola, and Concepcion. Concepcion, or Conchita as she was affectionately known, died of diphtheria when she was just eight years old. We can only speculate on the effect her death had on the 14 year old Picasso, but in later life he could not bear to be near people who were ill. After Picasso moved to Paris he made many friends, including the poet Guillaume Apollinaire and the strange writer Alfred Jarry, whose play *Ubu Roi* caused a riot when it opened in a Paris theater. Picasso's first love was Fernande Olivier whom he met when he moved in 1904 to the Bateau Lavoir (Laundry Barge), the name given to the apartment block in Montmartre, now famous for its association with so many artists.

PORTRAIT OF OLGA IN AN ARMCHAIR, 1917

In 1915, Picasso met pianist and composer Erik Satie. At the time Satie was composing music for a ballet called *Parade* for the famous impresario Sergei Diaghilev. The scenario was being written by a young man called Jean Cocteau who was to become firm friends with Picasso. Picasso agreed to paint the backdrops. The ballet was a disaster when it opened in Paris in 1917, despite being performed by the world-famous Russian Ballet. One of the dancers, Olga Khokhlova, daughter of a Russian general, caught Picasso's eye. In July, 1918, Olga and Picasso were married.

MA JOLIE, 1914

It was impossible for Picasso to be faithful to one woman. After Fernande walked out on Picasso one summer evening in 1911, he started courting a friend of Fernande named Marcelle Humbert. She was known as Eva Gouel and it appears that Picasso really did fall deeply in love with her. They moved to a studio in Montparnasse where they became devoted to each other. Picasso told his dealer that he loved Eva very much and would write it on his pictures. At this time the words *Ma Jolie* appeared on the painting. This was the name of a popular song and it appears that Picasso adopted it as an affectionate name (my pretty one) for Eva. This love was not to last. Tragically, Eva died from illness in 1915.

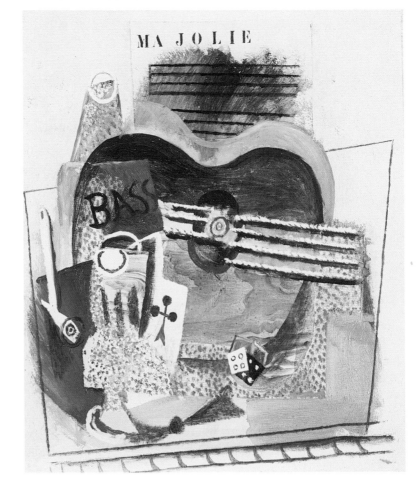

PAULO ON A DONKEY

On February 4, 1921, Olga gave birth to a son who was named Paulo. Picasso became, for a while, a doting father and always delighted in making sketches and paintings of their son such as the one shown here. By this time Picasso's work was very much in demand and sold for good prices. The family lacked for little in terms of material comforts but the stability of family life did not last. Dissatisfaction, perhaps by Olga as well as Picasso, appeared after a few short years.

THE LIFE OF PICASSO

~1881~
October 25 Picasso born in Malaga, Spain

~1895~
Sister Concepcion died aged eight

~1897~
Won gold medal in local art competition

~1900~
Moved to Paris

~1901~
Friend Casagemas commits suicide. "Blue Period" starts

THE LIFE OF PICASSO

~1904~
Met Fernande Olivier at the Bateau Lavoir. "Rose Period" starts

~1905~
Leo and Gertrude Stein become important patrons

~1907~
Painted *Les Demoiselles d'Avignon*

~1909~
Beginning of Cubism with Georges Braques

~1911~
Met and fell in love with Eva (Marcelle Humbert)

~1912~
Made first ever fabricated sculpture

~1914~
Start of World War I

~1915~
Eva died after a long illness

~1918~
Married Olga Khokhlova

~1921~
Birth of son Paulo

~1927~
Met Marie-Thérèse Walter

~1933~
Spanish Republic declared

~1934~
Hitler's Night of the Long Knives

~1935~
Separated from Olga. Birth of daughter Maya

MAYA WITH SAILOR DOLL, 1938

Maya inherited the blond hair and blue eyes of her mother. Picasso and Olga had separated but divorce was not possible, so Picasso could not marry Maya's mother. Picasso tried to sustain his life as a painter while Olga and son Paulo, and Marie Thérèse-Walter, and daughter Maya, lived in different parts of Paris. Meanwhile disturbing news about activities in Nazi Germany was emerging; and in 1936, Picasso's beloved Spain fell into civil war, the destruction aided by Nazi Germany. This portrait of Picasso's three year old daughter seems almost sinister. It is as if Picasso's work, by now filled with the horrors of war, cannot permit him to regain the innocence of the infant.

FRANÇOISE GILOT WITH PALOMA AND CLAUDE, 1954

Picasso had actually lived alone since the break-up with Olga, spending only weekends and holidays with Marie-Thérèse and short periods of time with Dora Maar. With Françoise Gilot, whom he met in 1943, he felt differently. Picasso first met Françoise when he was living in Nazi occupied Paris. By the time the war had ended in 1945, the 64 year old Picasso and Françoise, were living together in Antibes. In 1947 Françoise had a son, Claude. Shortly afterward they had another child, a girl they called Paloma.

THE ARTIST'S LIFE
NEW LOVES

By his mid-forties Picasso was truly a success. The impoverished days as a bohemian in the poor quarter of Paris had given way to the wealth and comfort of his villa on the Mediterranean coast, limousines with chauffeurs— and an unhappy marriage. In 1927, Picasso met a 17 year old girl on the streets of Paris. Her name was Marie-Thérèse Walter and they began a love affair soon afterward. Picasso was still married to Olga, so the meetings between Marie-Thérèse and Picasso were secret. His paintings at this time would have given the game away had Olga looked carefully, although it would seem this was something she had no interest in doing. Marie-Thérèse eventually (in 1935) had a child by Picasso whom they named Marie-Concepcion, Maya for short. Picasso's first daughter bore the name of the sister who had died 40 years earlier in Spain.

DORA MAAR, 1937

In 1936 Picasso's friend Paul Eluard introduced him to the photographer Dora Maar. She was *"inclined to storms—with thunder and lightning,"* according to a close friend. Picasso immediately fell for her. Picasso made this portrait of her at the same time that he was painting Marie-Thérèse and it appears that there was no conflict between the two women. For his part Picasso showed no sign of losing interest in Marie-Thérèse.

PORTRAIT OF MARIE-THÉRÈSE WALTER, 1939

Marie-Thérèse, remembering her first meeting with Picasso, recalled that: *"I was seventeen years old. I was an innocent young girl. I knew nothing—either of life or of Picasso. Nothing. I had gone to do some shopping at the Galeries Lafayette and Picasso saw me leaving the Metro. He simply took me by the arm and said: 'I am Picasso. You and I are going to do great things together.'"* The relationship remained secret for years. It is not known at what point Olga found out about Marie-Thérèse but probably in 1935, when Marie-Thérèse was pregnant with Maya. Legend has it that when a man called at Picasso and Olga's apartment to value the property as a basis for the separation settlement, Olga fainted.

LATER YEARS

Picasso's life with Françoise and the children lasted until 1953. Françoise decided she could no longer put up with his continual need to see both Marie-Thérèse and Dora Maar, apart from other occasional love affairs. She took the children with her to Paris. Françoise's memoirs recall Picasso with a certain bitterness, perhaps understandable: *"Picasso had insisted that I have children because I was not enough of a woman. And so I had them. One might have thought that I was, therefore, more of a woman, but it became clear that the whole question was for him a matter of complete indifference."* Picasso was alone once more, but Picasso could never be alone for long. After the departure of Françoise with Claude and Paloma he met Jacqueline Roque.

PICASSO IN HIS STUDIO WITH MODEL SYLVETTE DAVID

Picasso did not slow down toward the end of his life. He was still painting hundreds of canvases and making hundreds of prints every year. The writer Hélène Parmelin in her notes about Picasso's output, demonstrates his obsession with paint and canvas: *"On 2 March Picasso did 4 paintings; the painter and his model, and a green nude. On the 4th, a white nude plus 2 canvases with the painter's head. And on the 10th, a canvas of the painter alone in front of his painting. On the 13th, the nude holds a glass at arm's length, while the painter goes on working. On the 14th, the nude has left the scene, is sleeping perhaps. In any case the solitary painter is working at his easel in the studio. On the 25th the painter is still alone."* This obsession grew stronger as Picasso grew weaker. He painted right up to his death on April 8, 1973. Just months before his death and in his 92nd year, he said of a drawing: *"I did a drawing yesterday; and I think maybe I touched on something. It's not like anything I've done before."*

PICASSO WITH JACQUELINE ROQUE

Jacqueline Roque became Picasso's second wife. It would seem they met in the town of Vallauris in the South of France, where Picasso lived and worked in 1953. Olga's death in 1955 meant Picasso was free to marry and after some years with Jacqueline they were finally married in 1961. This photograph taken in 1957, shows them together in *La Californie*, the house they shared in Cannes. The huge house with its high-ceilinged rooms and views over Cannes bay became one enormous studio, where Picasso continued his immense production of paintings and sculptures.

Jacqueline had a daughter, Cathy, from a previous relationship. This photograph shows Picasso and Jacqueline with Cathy and Picasso's two children from his relationship with Françoise, Claude, and Paloma.

PORTRAIT OF JACQUELINE ROQUE WITH CROSSED ARMS, 1954

Jacqueline became the subject of his paintings, just as all his women had been throughout his life as an artist. He painted her obsessively, reducing the form to shapes and colors, lines and textures. Life at *La Californie* was full and varied as Picasso's political interests (he had long been a member of the French Communist Party) sparked debate when Soviet tanks rolled into Hungary. Film stars such as Yves Montand and Gary Cooper visited, as did old friends such as Jean Cocteau.

THE LIFE OF PICASSO

~1936~
Met Dora Maar

~1937~
April 26 Germans bomb Spanish town of Guernica. Painted *Guernica* mural for Spanish republican Pavilion

~1939~
Beginning of World War II

~1943~
Met Françoise Gilot

~1945~
End of World War II

~1947~
Birth of son Claude

~1949~
Birth of daughter Paloma

~1953~
Françoise moved out with Claude and Paloma

~1961~
Married Jacqueline Roque

~1967~
Picasso painting sells for the highest ever price for work by a living artist

~1973~
Picasso died on April 8

~1981~
Sale of self-portrait for five and a half million dollars breaks all records.

FAMILY OF SALTIMBANQUES, 1905

The Saltimbanques is almost a roll-call of all the circus characters in one painting. It was the largest canvas Picasso had attempted to date, over 6 ft 6 in (2 meters) square, and recaptures the full range of colors lost in his "Blue Period." There is an overwhelming seriousness about the characters in *Saltimbanques* quite at odds with the public perception of their roles as entertainers. As with his other pictures of this time we do not know the significance of the group but it is interesting to note that a little girl with a basket of flowers is holding the harlequin's—Picasso's—hand. She would be about the same age as Picasso's lost sister, Concepcion.

APOLLINAIRE AND FERNANDE

Some have suggested that the fat jester (right) represents his friend Apollinaire and the seated woman (left) Picasso's lover Fernande Olivier.

18

The figure wearing the harlequin's costume is Picasso himself.

WHAT DO THE PAINTINGS SAY?

From 1901 to 1904, Picasso's paintings became predominantly blue, and as a consequence this period has become known as his "Blue Period." The reasons why his work became dominated by one color are speculative, but certainly the loss of his friend Carlos Casagemas had a profound effect upon Picasso, which in turn affected his painting. Casagemas was a fellow artist who had traveled to Paris with Picasso in 1900. They had lodged together in Montmartre but when Picasso returned to Spain at Christmas, Casagemas stayed with his new-found lover Germaine. The affair was short-lived and tragic, ending with Casagemas shooting himself in the head in the back room of a Parisian wine shop in February of the following year. *It was thinking about Casagemas that got me started painting in blue,* Picasso admitted in later life.

THE TRAGEDY, 1903

Picasso was deeply upset by the death of his friend. In addition to his sadness he was poverty-stricken and was having little success with his painting. He spent much of his time in Spain, locked away and devoting his time to painting. When he did make periodical visits to Paris he no longer found a market for the paintings that he had when first in the city. He was trying to make a memorial to his friend, but was continually dissatisfied with his efforts. There is no doubt that *The Tragedy* speaks of the terrible loss of Casagemas, even though we do not know who the characters are and why they stand huddled on the beach.

Picasso later said: *"I certainly didn't intend to paint symbols; I simply painted images that rose in front of my eyes; it's for others to find a hidden meaning in them."* The style and overall blue hue are however typical of the paintings he made during this period.

ACROBAT ON A BALL, 1905

Picasso had spent much of the time since Casagemas's death in Barcelona, but in April 1904, he returned to Paris where he was to stay. He moved into the Bateau Lavoir where he met Fernande Olivier who described Picasso as: *"small, black, thick-set, restless, disquieting,with eyes dark, profound, piercing, strange, almost staring... a thick lock of hair, black, and shining, slashed across his intelligent and obstinate forehead."* His spirits lifted and his paintings became full of harlequins and circus people. The blues changed to pinks. The time from 1904 to 1905, has become known as the "Rose Period" or "Circus Period." Picasso and his friends met once a week at the Circus Medrano where they went behind the scenes. Picasso made friends with the harlequins, jugglers, and strolling players. His paintings of the subject, however, are composed in an almost classical manner.

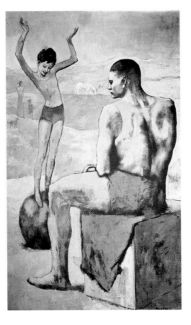

The seated figure in *Acrobat on a Ball* is painted in a style which is more like Michelangelo than his contemporary artists.

WHAT DO THE PAINTINGS SAY?

By 1906, Picasso was beginning to get noticed in the right circles. The Parisian art critics were now paying attention to the 25 year old artist whose exciting works were rivaling Matisse. In the summer of that year Picasso and Fernande left Paris for the tiny village of Gosol in the Pyrenees. So inaccessible was it that their luggage had to be carried on mule-back. The pictures he painted in Gosol indicated that he was not continuing with the attractive compositions of the "Rose Period," but experimenting with a new style. A typhoid epidemic caused Picasso and Fernande to leave Gosol later that summer. Picasso carried back to Paris his paintings, sketches, and ideas that had formed in the remote mountain village. During the spring and summer of 1907, Picasso worked on a painting which was to break with the artistic traditions that had dominated western art for the previous 500 years. This painting was initially called *Le Bordel* (the Bordello) but became known as *Les Demoiselles d'Avignon* (the young ladies of Avignon).

AFRICAN MASK

Art from different cultures began to influence Picasso and his fellow artists. Matisse had bought an African mask and Derain had visited the British Museum collection of African art. Iberian Primitive art was on show at the Louvre at the time, some of which, apparently, had been stolen and turned up in the artist's colony where Picasso worked. The violently misshapen and striped faces of the figures on the right in *Les Demoiselles d'Avignon* owe much to these new influences.

A few of Picasso's friends and acquaintances saw *Les Demoiselles d'Avignon*. None could understand it, not even his close friends. Picasso felt isolated and to make matters worse he had separated from Fernande. The young art dealer Daniel Kahnweiler seemed to have recognized the painting's worth, but said: *"The picture... struck everyone as something mad and monstrous."*

BREAKING THE RULES OF ART
LES DEMOISELLES D'AVIGNON, 1907

The great developments in art during the Renaissance in the 15th century led artists to represent their subject in a realistic way. Studies of human anatomy and the employment of perspective helped artists to paint pictures which "tricked" the viewers into thinking that what they saw was a real extension of the world, not a flat surface. This was of course an illusion. These artistic conventions continued into the 20th century. One painting more than any other served to bring about a change in this tradition, and that was *Les Demoiselles d'Avignon*. It was the prologue to the movement called Cubism which was to break the Renaissance tradition and prepare the way for the art of the 20th century.

Picasso made countless sketches for the painting which was to be the biggest yet, over 6 ft 6 in (2 meters) square. The painting started out with a sailor and a student in a brothel. As Picasso worked away at the picture, it gradually changed over a period of months during the summer of 1907. The student and sailor made way for more women and, importantly, the influence of "Primitive" art makes a dramatic impact. The figures jump violently from the background. The angularity and unharmonious composition makes the eye travel unhappily across the picture, leaping from one distorted face to another. The radical departure from traditional painting is evident; no longer can the viewer try to understand the picture as an extension of the real world, there is no perspective to give the painting depth, there is no attempt at illusion. Picasso has made a new type of painting.

BOTTLE AND PIPE, 1915

With this painting, made in 1915, Picasso is very close to completely abstract art. Braque had stated that: *"when the fragmentation of objects appeared in my paintings around 1910, it was a technique for getting closer to the object."* The normal everyday objects found in the cafés of Paris, such as newspapers, were now not only the subject of Picasso's paintings, but were sometimes physically part of the painting (collage). Picasso was recreating the world around him but not in a way that imitated reality.

VIOLIN, 1911/12

The Cubist style of painting attempted to display frontally, parts of a depicted object that might be observed from any angle. Painting in this way would display all facets of an object flattened out to be seen from the front. Braque's manner of painting literally squared everything—houses, trees, landscapes—into cubes. Picasso's paintings sought to explode the object, to take it apart visually in order to see what it was made of, to "de-construct" what he saw. This painting of a violin, which was made in 1911, demonstrates the technique. Many views of the same object are displayed on the flat plane of the picture surface.

Picasso has chosen to emphasize certain parts of the violin more than others. The clef shaped cut-out from the front of the violin sound box is prominent, as is the wood grain. The bridge and strings move diagonally from left, and upward, from bottom center. Not only has the violin been flattened but Picasso has chosen what he considers to be the most important visual elements of the object and accentuated them while allowing others, including the true shape of the violin, to be lost.

WHAT DO THE PAINTINGS SAY?

After painting *Les Demoiselles d'Avignon*, Picasso turned the canvas to face the wall. It had not been well received and was not to get a full public airing until several years later when it was received with indifference. Picasso was well aware of the importance of his painting as was another artist, Georges Braque, who had not openly praised the picture, but had been impressed. Braque was a great follower of Cézanne who had taken landscape painting one step further by beginning to turn everything into geometric shapes. Six paintings submitted to the *Salon* by Braque in the autumn of 1907 were reviewed by Matisse, who was on the selection jury. Matisse commented that Braque had reduced everything to *petit cubes* (little cubes). The critic Louis Vauxcelles described them as "Cubist," and the name stuck. Braque and Picasso watched each other's work carefully. Following on from *Les Demoiselles d'Avignon* Picasso's work developed a distinctly Cubist style.

BOTTLE OF PERNOD, 1912

From 1907, Picasso, Braque, and others, particularly Leger and Gris, continued to explore the new Cubist view of the world. Picasso appears now to have been liberated from the tyranny of having to represent what he saw in the traditional way, and was moving quickly toward non-representational or *abstract* art. It is still possible to make out what is depicted in *Bottle of Pernod*. A bottle and glass stand on a table. Advertising signs full of words fill the background. Picasso shows as much, perhaps more, interest in the flat words as he does in the three dimensional objects, and paints them with equal emphasis.

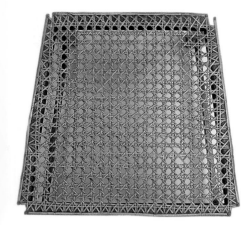

HOW WERE THEY MADE?

Picasso made another invention in 1912, which was to have an enormous impact. When making a painting of a still-life of a café scene he decided to glue a piece of oil-cloth with a chair caning overprint onto the canvas. Braque followed Picasso's lead and also started to employ the technique called "collage." The paintings that followed incorporated more "real" objects such as newspapers, rope—anything that could successfully be stuck onto the canvas. In their pursuit of reality, the artists were making the paintings real with real things instead of representing them through the medium of paint.

With Cubism, came a new approach to art. Both Picasso and Braque were pushing to the limits the way in which objects could be represented in a picture. This new art was no longer readily understandable by a wider public. They could not share the "illusion" of reality that earlier artists had created on the flat picture plane, because it had now been destroyed and replaced by the artist's personal view of that reality. The "personal" view of Picasso and Braque no longer relied on existing artistic conventions of representation. The two artists spurred each other onward and upward. As Braque was later to say: *"we were like two climbers roped together on a mountain."*
In 1912, they started making cardboard models of objects to assist with the paintings. Picasso suddenly realized that he was making Cubist sculpture, a totally new approach to the art form. Instead of carving from stone or modeling from clay he was constructing from sheet metal.

Picasso made clay figures and ceramic pots which he painted in bright colors.

Picasso's interest in sculpture continued throughout his life. He was particularly fascinated by *objets trouvés* (found objects). He would delight in taking everyday objects that he found lying around and with the minimum of intervention turn them into something else. An example of this was the *Bull's Head* which he made by fixing the handlebars of a bicycle to the top of a bicycle's saddle. When he was praised for seeing a remarkable likeness in such mundane objects he said *"That's not enough. It should be possible to take a bit of wood and find that it's a bird."*

Picasso was happy creating things. When he was not painting he was making sculptures using ordinary materials lying around the house or studio.

THE GOAT, 1950

The realization that ordinary materials such as cardboard, sheet metal, and wire, could be turned into art was an enormous step in the progress of 20th-century art. Until that time it had not entered into anyone's head to make a sculpture from everyday objects and found materials. Picasso's *Goat* demonstrates what is possible; a palm forms the spine; a wicker basket, the swollen belly; ceramic jars, the udders; a metal lid folded in two, the genitals. After casting in plaster the final piece is realized in bronze, the traditional sculptor's material.

FAMOUS IMAGES

In 1936, Picasso's beloved Spain was plunged into civil war. The Republic of Spain, ruled by a weak Popular Government, faced an uprising from the right wing military generals, led by Franco. Spain became a battleground for the international forces of communism and fascism. In January, 1937, the Spanish ambassador in Paris asked Picasso to contribute a mural painting for the Spanish pavilion of the Paris World's Fair. Picasso was not enthusiastic about the request, and gave a non-committal reply. Guernica changed everything.

FRANCISCO FRANCO

After his victory, General Franco ruled Spain through the war and for 30 years thereafter. Although Picasso was keen that *Guernica* would one day find a home in Spain his condition was that: *"the painting shall be turned over to the government of the Spanish Republic the day the Republic is restored in Spain."* As years passed this clearly would not happen. It was later changed to: *"when public liberties are re-established in Spain."* After Franco's death in 1975, new calls for the painting's return were made. Picasso's heirs (Picasso had died in 1973) and the Museum of Modern Art in New York finally agreed, and *Guernica* was installed in the Prado in Madrid.

A howling mother carries her dead child in her arms.

A dead soldier still clutching his broken sword lies across the base of the picture.

On April 26, 1937, Republican troops gathered in the Basque town of Guernica in Northern Spain. Franco enlisted the help of the German Nazi Luftwaffe (air-force), who were keen to try out their new planes and had three squadrons stationed nearby. The squadrons were manned by German pilots who wore Spanish uniforms and were known as the Condor Legion. The bombing of the virtually undefended Guernica by the Nazi planes completely destroyed the town, and hardly a building was left standing. After the bombing, the Nazis machine-gunned civilians as they attempted to flee. As news of the massacre spread the world was stunned into silence.

AN OCEAN OF MISERY AND DEATH

When on April 27, news of Guernica reached Picasso through the world press only 27 days remained until the opening of the World's Fair. On April 30, the first photographs of the atrocity appeared. On May 1, Picasso started his sketches for the mural for the Spanish pavilion at the Fair. He no longer doubted what he should do. While working on the mural he said: *"The war in Spain is a war of reaction—against the people, against liberty. My whole life as an artist has been a continual struggle against reaction, and the death of art. In the picture I'm now painting—which I shall call Guernica—and in all my recent work, I am expressing my horror of the military caste which is now plunging Spain into an ocean of misery and death."*

Picasso referred to the bull as brutality and darkness, and the dying horse as the people.

Here is a figure who appears to be consumed by the flames of a burning building.

A fleeing woman runs beneath another who looks on in horror, arm outstretched, clutching a lamp.

GUERNICA, 1937

On May 11, Picasso started sketching out the composition for the painting on a canvas 11 ft 6 in by over 25 ft (3.5 by 7.5 meters). The painting, which was made entirely in black and white and shades of gray, could not be finished and exhibited in the Spanish pavilion until June. Picasso had created one of the most enduring images of the 20th century and possibly his best known work. It was however criticized—predictably by the fascists who called it "degenerate"—but also by the communists who called the painting: *"anti-social and entirely foreign to a healthy proletarian outlook."*

PHOTOGRAPH OF PICASSO BY MAN RAY

In July 1938, Picasso moved to the south coast of France for the summer. He stayed in an apartment lent to him by artist Man Ray and was planning to stay throughout the summer painting as usual. Picasso's stay was cut short by news of the death of a friend which took him back to Paris. As the prospect of war appeared to grow stronger he hurried to join Marie-Thérèse and Maya in the Atlantic coastal town of Royan. He stayed there while the German forces marched into Paris on June 14, 1940, and when Royan itself was occupied by the German army shortly thereafter. Picasso then decided to return to occupied Paris where he was to stay until the end of the war despite being invited by the Americans to move to the United States. Fellow artist Matisse had already made the same decision, writing: *"If everyone did his job as Picasso and I are doing ours, all of this wouldn't be happening."*

WEEPING WOMAN, 1937

To the occupying German forces Picasso's work was a prime example of "degenerate" art. This was art which did not conform to the dull standards of Nazi culture, which only accepted traditional representative art. Paintings such as the *Weeping Woman*, which was based on Dora Maar but was a painting about grief and sorrow at the terrible occurrences in Europe, was dismissed as rubbish by the Nazis. The Fauvist painter Maurice Vlaminck took the opportunity to attack Picasso, no doubt hoping to curry favor with the German authorities. Vlaminck commented: *"Pablo Picasso is guilty of dragging French painting to a mortal impasse, a state of indescribable confusion. From 1900 to 1930 he has led painting to negation, impotence, and death... The only thing Picasso absolutely cannot do is a Picasso which is a Picasso."* However, Picasso was not in danger and in time Marie-Thérèse and Maya joined him in Paris.

BULL'S HEAD ON A TABLE, 1942

Picasso painted this picture in the darkest hours of World War II. Picasso's Jewish friends such as Max Jacob were rounded up by the Nazis. They were not to survive. The bull's head appears to be presented on a clean white tablecloth as if served as a meal. The black and white rendering of the head and horns is splattered with red paint and the tablecloth is smeared with red. It is impossible to look at this violent still life without thinking of the animal brutality of war.

FAMOUS IMAGES

The devastation in Spain was a cause of anger and torment for Picasso. He feared for his family in Malaga, which had fallen to the fascists. On January 13, 1938, just days before Franco's army marched into Barcelona, Picasso's mother died. Hitler's forces were poised to strike at Germany's neighbors and Picasso feared for the safety of his own family in France. In July 1938, Picasso sent Marie-Thérèse and daughter Maya away from Paris to the coast. On July 19 Picasso wrote: *"My love, I have just received your letter. And I have written several to you, which you must by now have received. I love you more every day. You mean everything to me. And I will sacrifice everything for you, and for our love, which shall last forever...*

My own tears would mean nothing to me if I could stop you from shedding even one. I love you. Kiss Maria, our daughter."

MAN WITH A LAMB, 1943

Picasso made almost 100 preparatory drawings for this sculpture, starting in 1942 and continuing throughout the year and into 1943. The figure holding a lamb is a return to both classical and Christian imagery, referring to human values and the lamb of God. The figure, which stands over 6 ft (2 meters) high, was finally modeled in clay and then cast in 1944—a difficult process given the shortage of bronze in occupied Paris.

THE ARTIST'S INFLUENCE

THE AUDIENCE FOR THE PICTURES

THE AMERICAN PATRON

In 1905, a young wealthy American art collector named Leo Stein bought two of Picasso's paintings. Stein wrote of Picasso at the time: *"a young Spaniard... whom I consider a genius of very considerable magnitude and one of the most notable draughtsmen living."* Leo was living in Paris with his sister, Gertrude, and the couple later visited Picasso in his studio. Picasso proposed painting a portrait of Gertrude for which Picasso insisted Gertrude posed over 90 times during the course of the painting. Leo and Gertrude Stein became lifelong friends and their patronage was extremely important in helping to establish Picasso's reputation. Before her death in 1947, Gertrude wrote of Picasso: *"He alone among painters did not set himself the problem of expressing truths which all the world can see, but the truth which only he can see."*

The detail above (of Gertrude Stein) is from Renato Guttuso's painting Totenmahl, a tribute to Picasso (see page 34).

Picasso was fortunate to find people who were ready to support him from a relatively early time in his life. When first in Paris an art dealer, Ambroise Vollard, expressed an interest in Picasso's work and exhibited his paintings in his gallery. This show, in 1901, was Picasso's first real exhibition. Vollard and Picasso remained firm friends with Vollard representing Picasso's work during his early career. It was the age when art dealers were making an increasing impact and helping to shape the world of art. Another young dealer, Daniel Kahnweiler, had recently started his business with a sum of money from his wealthy father. Kahnweiler heard about Picasso's *Les Demoiselles d'Avignon* and tried to buy it, but Picasso would sell only his preparatory studies. Competition from dealers soon brought Picasso success. Apart from some difficult times when he was first living in Paris, Picasso was quickly able to support himself by the sale of his work. For an artist to support himself, particularly as a young man, is unusual. Artists have struggled to make ends meet throughout the history of art, often relying on private income to subsidize their art. Picasso's extraordinary genius was recognized instantly, providing him and his extended family an income which grew over the years into a considerable financial fortune.

Costu

Color print of a watercolor by Picasso, 1917.

d'Acrobate du ballet "PARADE"
Aquarelle de Picasso.

LA PARADE

Picasso's friendship with the composer Erik Satie led to an invitation to work on designs for a modern ballet, *La Parade*, which opened in Paris in 1917. Sergei Diaghilev, who had founded one of the greatest international ballet companies, the Ballets Russes, had commissioned Satie to compose the music for the ballet. The young writer and playwright Jean Cocteau was writing the scenario (story). Cocteau was aware of Picasso's circus paintings and was planning a ballet based on circus figures. Picasso's influence created a new approach. He designed "cubist" costumes constructed from card which made the dancers look like his cubist paintings. Other costumes were based on his favorite theme, the harlequin.

*Portrait of Diaghilev
by Leon Bakst, 1906.*

A letter of the time from Satie hints at some of the problems caused by Picasso's involvement with the ballet designs: *"Parade is turning into something better, behind Cocteau's back. Picasso's ideas I find even better than those of our Jean: what a malheur! I am for Picasso, and Jean doesn't know it. What to do? Picasso tells me to work with Jean's text while he, Picasso, is using another, his own."* The performance was a disaster in popular terms, but has become a landmark in the history of ballet, one of the first truly modern pieces.

(right) Jean Cocteau drawing Maria Calvi.

31

YO PICASSO, 1901

In 1967, an early "Blue Period" picture sold for $532,000, the highest price ever paid for a work of a living artist. This 1901 self-portrait called *Yo Picasso* (I Picasso) came up for auction in 1981, just 8 years after Picasso's death. It fetched a record price of over five and a half million dollars. Picasso could accurately be described as a *"legend in his own lifetime."* His early critical success established his reputation. This was to grow steadily as demand from collectors and dealers further enhanced his standing. It is worth recalling, however, that Picasso had always been an obsessive painter, even from early childhood. He painted because he had to. Success was a by-product of that obsession.

WHAT THE CRITICS SAY

The first review of Picasso's work appeared in the Paris press in 1900, when his paintings were exhibited in Vollard's gallery. The critic Félicien Fagus wrote in the magazine La Revue Blanche: *"Picasso is a painter, absolutely and beautifully... one can easily see many an influence apart from his own great ancestry; Delacroix, Manet, Monet, van Gogh, Pissaro, Toulouse-Lautrec, Degas... each one a passing phase... his passionate surge forward has not yet left him the leisure to forge for himself a personal style."* This was certainly praise for a 19 year old beginning to make his way in the world. Picasso did forge a personal style, but it was one that was always open to ideas and influences. His creative genius made his work too elusive, too varied to label as one style. The furore surrounding his 1907 painting *Les Demoiselles d'Avignon* brought criticism from not only the professional critics but even from his closest friends. Nevertheless, Picasso had absolute faith in what he was doing. Today the critics recognize that the painting was revolutionary and affected the course of 20th-century art.

HOMAGE TO PICASSO

Picasso's legacy of work is vast. Picasso Museums now exist both in his native Spain (in Barcelona) and in his adopted France (in Paris). The Picasso Museum in Paris now houses the famous *Maya with Sailor Doll* along with other works by Picasso.

LANDSCAPE NEAR CANNES AT TWILIGHT, 1960

The art historians and critics have been dismissive of Picasso's later work. Many accounts and reviews of his art disregard most of his work from the late 1940s onward, despite the fact that he continued painting until his death in 1973. Picasso was, of course, overtaken by the many new movements in art to which critics turned their attention. It is easy to forget that Picasso's life spanned virtually a century and that some of the greatest changes in the history of art occurred in this period. When he started painting, the Impressionists were the dominant force; when he died Pop Art was already a thing of the past. When his last pictures were exhibited, after his death, the critics called them "incoherent scribblings," and said they were the result of "senility." Who can tell what people will make of them 100 years from now?

DOVE OF PEACE

After World War II, Picasso's political sympathies were with the communists, and he joined the French Communist Party. He went to the World Peace Congress in Poland in 1948, where he was met with the charge from the Soviets that: *"His works are a sickly apology for capitalist aesthetics that provoke the indignation of the simple people... his every canvas deforms man, his body, and face."* Nevertheless, he was happy for his picture of a pigeon to be used on a poster for the "World Congress for the Partisans of Peace," sponsored by the French Communist Party in 1949. It was not exactly a dove, but it would do as the "dove of peace." While the congress was in session, Picasso's daughter was born and christened Paloma, the Spanish for dove.

TOTENMAHL *Renato Guttuso*

After Picasso's death in 1973, the Italian artist Renato Guttuso painted a tribute to
him in the manner of a final meal or last supper, with characters from paintings
across all periods of Picasso's paintings and sculptures appearing round the table.

ADVERTISING STYLE

One of the most memorable aspects of Picasso's
work is the re-arrangement of facial features
to make them appear on one flat plane rather
than as we come to expect them to look in
life, or in conventional art which tries to
mirror life. Picasso's challenge to how we
see things caused him to depart from traditional
representation and was part of his development
of what we call today Analytical Cubism.
Picasso is famous for pointing out that the
untutored eye of a young child will draw
things how he or she sees them—often like
Picasso's flat faced portrait—and that the
freshness of observation so sought after by
artists is destroyed by teaching. This 1930s
poster for Shell, recalls the compositional
style of Picasso's cubist work.

THE ARTIST'S INFLUENCE
A LASTING IMPRESSION

Picasso is arguably the most important artist of the 20th century. He produced a huge number of paintings, drawings, prints, and sculptures and most museums of modern art throughout the world have examples of his work. Today art historians place his name alongside those of Giotto and Michelangelo because, like them, Picasso's work represents a radical change in the course of Western art. He is said to have freed painters from "the tyranny of representational art," meaning that he made it possible for those that followed to develop non-representational— abstract—art. It is for abstract art that the 20th century will be remembered, and it is Picasso who helped make abstract art possible. The huge range of Picasso's work encompasses many different styles. He evolved Cubism with fellow artist Braque; he invented Collage; he helped evolve Surrealism and, of course, Abstract art. In later life Picasso considered himself part of the long-standing tradition of painters such as Velazquez and Manet, rather than the new generation whose careers could never bear comparison with Picasso, the master.

CONTINUING FAME

Picasso's works are still actively traded in the art dealing rooms today. When a painting from an important period in his life comes up for sale it will command many millions of dollars. However, thousands of his drawings, prints, and lesser paintings frequently change hands through the dealers. The theft of one of Picasso's works made newspaper headlines. The incident underlines not only how valuable even the smaller Picasso pictures are, but the things some people will do to own a picture by the master of the 20th century.

AFTER GUERNICA

A major exhibition of Picasso's work was held at the National Gallery in Berlin in 1992. This exhibition concentrated on his artistic output after the world famous *Guernica*, painted in 1937. Although it is considered that Picasso's influence was most profound during the earlier part of his career and that art historians see *Guernica* as his last great work, we should not overlook the paintings that followed. This picture was painted when Picasso was 91 years old.

Musicians, 1972.

DID YOU KNOW?
FASCINATING FACTS ABOUT THE ARTIST AND THE TIMES IN WHICH HE WORKED

• When Picasso was born, he was not breathing. Thinking he was stillborn, the midwife left him on a table and went to care for his mother. His uncle, Dr. Don Salvador, looked at the puny baby and puffed cigar smoke into his face. The tiny baby coughed, spluttered, and yelled in anger—Picasso had arrived in the world.

• At the age of fourteen, Picasso completed his first major painting that featured a portrait of his father, mother, and younger sister kneeling at an altar, called *First Communion*. The work shows an understanding of color, composition, and technique that many mature artists could not achieve.

• At school or art college, Picasso always resented being told what to do by the teachers and was often disobedient.

• Noticeably more talented than any other student and even than most of his teachers, from an early age, Picasso could work proficiently with any medium, including watercolors, oils, pastels, charcoal, pencil, and ink.

• When he was sixteen, Picasso went to Madrid's Royal Academy, the main art school in Spain. To his parents' dismay, he left within a year as there was nothing new that the teachers could teach him.

• While in Madrid, Picasso visited the Prado art gallery and studied paintings by the great Spanish masters of the past, including Velázquez, Goya, Zurbarán, and El Greco.

• During his first years in Paris, Picasso shared an apartment with a new friend, a young writer called Max Jacob. They were so poor that they could only afford one bed. So Jacob worked during the day and slept in the bed at night and Picasso worked at night and slept in the bed during the day.

• Because of the dampness and odd shape, Jacob nicknamed Picasso's rented studio the "Bateau-Lavoir," meaning laundry boat.

• From 1900, Picasso made eight trips back and forth between Spain and France, finally settling in Paris in 1904.

• When Picasso was in his "Rose Period" and concentrated on painting the circus performers he saw at the Circus Medrano, he identified with the character of Harlequin—the unsmiling clown—because he amused people and pretended to be happy, even if he felt miserable inside.

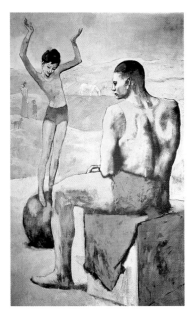

• During World War II, the Germans occupied France. Many of Picasso's friends were arrested, forced into hiding, or killed. Picasso was not afraid of them, however. One day, when a German officer saw a photo of his painting *Guernica* showing the atrocities of war, the officer asked him "Did you do this?" Picasso replied, "No, you did."

• In 1946, Picasso visited a pottery exhibition near his home in the South of France. Fascinated by the ceramics that had been produced there for centuries, he set about learning the techniques. Within a year, using those age-old methods, he produced two thousand pieces of pottery.

• Several of Picasso's paintings that have been sold at auction rank among the most expensive paintings in the world.

• In 1909, when Diaghilev took the Ballet Russes (Russian Ballet) to Paris, it created a sensation. The Parisians loved it, for the music, costumes, sets, and choreography. Picasso was no exception and when he designed the costumes and sets for the ballet *Parade*, he had a new burst of creativity. He continued working with the Ballets Russes for several other ballets and all were equally popular.

• In 1911 when the Mona Lisa was stolen from the Louvre, Picasso was taken in for questioning by the police as a suspect. He was later released without charge.

• Whenever Picasso changed his girlfriend or wife, he seemed to change his artistic style at the same time!

• In 1924, Picasso became interested in Surrealism that explored dreams and had been inspired by Sigmund Freud's discoveries about the power of our subconscious minds. Picasso was never an official member of the movement, but he used several of the ideas in his work.

• As the Nazi Party rose to power in Germany and threatened the rest of Europe, Picasso began painting Minotaurs. He had always painted bulls—as a symbol of Spain—but the Minotaur, a mythical bull, was his way of symbolizing social concern.

SUMMARY TIMELINE OF
THE ARTIST & HIS CONTEMPORARIES

THE LIFE OF PICASSO

~1881~
In the year of Picasso's birth, the Russian ballerina Anna Pavlova is also born; in Paris, the sixth Impressionist exhibition is held

~1884~
The artists Beckmann and Modigliani and Picasso's sister Dolores, known as Lola are born

~1885~
Cézanne paints *The Bather*; a cholera epidemic occurs in Spain

~1887~
Picasso's sister Concepcíon and the artists Juan Gris, Marc Chagall, and Georgia O'Keeffe are born

~1891~
Picasso moves with his family from Málaga to La Coruña on the north-west coast of Spain; the artist Max Ernst is born

~1895~
When seven-year-old Concepcíon dies, the family moves to Barcelona; Picasso enters La Llotja Academy of Art where his father teaches

~1897~
Picasso begins studying at Madrid's Royal Academy, but leaves within months; *Science and Charity* receives an honorary mention at the National Exhibition of Fine Arts in Madrid and a Gold Medal at an exhibition in Málaga; the first underground passenger train in America opens in Boston

~1900~
Picasso's first exhibition is held in Barcelona and he visits Paris with his friend Casagemas and meets Max Jacob; the Paris Exposition Universelle is held to celebrate achievements of the past century

~1903~
Gauguin and Pissarro die; Picasso lives in Barcelona and produces over fifty paintings in his Blue Period; the first teddy bear is made, named after President Theodore ("Teddy") Roosevelt; the Wright brothers take

the first powered flight; the artist Mark Rothko is born

~1905~
Matisse and friends are called Les Fauves; Picasso exhibits his first Rose Period works; Christian Dior is born

~1907~
In the year that *Les Demoiselles d'Avignon* shocks his fellow artists, Picasso meets Georges Braque; Daniel Kahnweiler becomes his art dealer; Frida Kahlo is born

~1910~
Two years after he first teams up with Braque, Picasso produces his first Cubist sculpture and illustrates a novel by Max Jacob; George V ascends the British throne; Portugal becomes a republic; Winslow Homer dies; Matisse paints *Music*

~1914~
At the start of World War I, Braque is called to join the

French Army and his collaboration with Picasso ends

~1916~

Picasso's friend, writer Jean Cocteau, introduces him to Diaghilev, founder of the Ballets Russes; they ask Picasso to design costumes and stage sets; Monet begins painting his huge Water Lily paintings; the artists Franz Marc, Thomas Eakins, and Odilon Redon die

~1917~

The artists Degas, J. W. Waterhouse, and Rodin die; America severs diplomatic relations with Germany; the Russian Revolution occurs; Picasso travels to Rome to work on the ballet Parade and meets Olga Khokhlova; the photographer Irving Penn is born

~1918~

World War I ends; Picasso has a joint exhibition with Matisse in Paris and meets writers James Joyce and Marcel Proust; over 25 million people die in a Spanish Flu pandemic

~1922~

With Olga and Paulo, Picasso visits Dinard on the north-west coast of France and paints large ladies and mythological creatures

inspired by Classicism and Neoclassicism; Howard Carter and Lord Carnarvon become the first people to enter the Pharaoh Tutankhamun's tomb in over 3,000 years

~1925~

Picasso exhibits with the first Surrealist group exhibition and several of his works are published in a Surrealist journal

~1928~

Picasso begins working with metal sculpture and meets Salvador Dalí

~1935~

Marie-Thérèse gives birth to their daughter Maya

and Olga leaves him; he produces etchings called *Minotauromachy*; Elvis is born; Persia is renamed Iran

~1936~

In the year that Picasso meets Dora Maar, he is made honorary director of the Prado Museum in Madrid; the Spanish Civil War begins; in Britain, King Edward VIII abdicates

~1939~

Despite the outbreak of World War II, Picasso refuses to leave France; his mother dies in Barcelona; the Museum of Modern Art in New York holds a successful exhibition of his work; Franco wins the Spanish Civil War

~1945~

At the end of World War II, Picasso begins experimenting with printing; penicillin is developed

~1947~

Picasso, Françoise, and their new baby Claude move to Provence where Picasso begins working in ceramics

~1954~

Picasso's friends Matisse and Derain die; the first colored television set is made

~1963~

The Museu Picasso opens in Barcelona; in America, President John F. Kennedy is assassinated; Picasso's friends, Braque and Cocteau, die

~1973~

In the year of Picasso's death, the first space station, Skylab, is launched

WHAT DID HE SAY?

Here are some of the things Picasso said about art:

• "When we discovered Cubism, we did not aim to discover Cubism. We only wanted to express what was in us"

• "All children are artists. The problem is how to remain an artist once he grows up"

• "Are we to paint what's on the face, what's inside the face, or what's behind it?"

• "Art is the lie that enables us to realize the truth"

• "Computers are useless. They can only give you answers"

• "Give me a museum and I'll fill it"

• "Only put off until tomorrow what you are willing to die having left undone"

• "One must act in painting as in life, directly"

• "Some painters transform the sun into a yellow spot, others transform a yellow spot into the sun"

• "The world today doesn't make sense, so why should I paint pictures that do?"

• "There is no abstract art. You must always start with something. Afterwards you can remove all traces of reality"

• "I paint objects as I think them, not as I see them"

• "Inspiration exists, but it has to find us working"

• "It took me four years to paint like Raphael, but a lifetime to paint like a child"

• "We don't grow older, we just grow riper"

• "My mother said to me, 'If you are a soldier, you will become a general. If you are a monk, you will become the Pope.' Instead, I was a painter, and became Picasso"

A WORK IN CLOSE-UP

This was the first work of art by an established artist to use collage. Once again, Picasso had brought in an unexpected and innovative element to fine art, moving Cubism into another phase. In showing more than one view, Cubism was exploring how to show more of the subject, but in effect it all had to be worked out. This was one of a series of oval shaped still lifes that he painted in the spring of 1912.

The picture includes a café table and wicker chair with objects on it, including a magazine and a wineglass.

Picasso primed the canvas in off-white paint and then added layers of wet paint for the image.

The lettering was painted without a stencil. "JOU" indicates the word "journal" and also the French word for play: *jouer*.

White impasto paint was added in places to create texture.

Lines show where the objects are viewed from different angles— this is how originally, the style became called "Cubism."

The palette includes yellow, ocher, black, white, and sienna—the only bright color is lemon yellow.

Oil-cloth with chair caning overprint has been glued to the canvas and painted on, so that it becomes part of the picture.

The frame, made with actual rope, glued around the edge of the canvas, is part of the image.

Still Life with Chair-Caning, 1912,
oil and oilcloth on canvas, with rope frame,
11 x 14 in/27 x 35 cm,
Musée Picasso, Paris, France

WHERE TO SEE THIS ARTIST'S WORKS IN THE USA

There are plenty of places to see Picasso's work across the USA. Not all works are permanently on display though, so it is a good idea to check before visiting.

The Art Institute
of Chicago,
Chicago, Illinois
(www.artic.edu)

The Detroit Institute
of Arts,
Detroit, Michigan
(www.dia.org)

Fine Arts Museums
of San Francisco,
San Francisco, California
(www.famsf.org)

The Guggenheim Museum,
New York
(www.guggenheim.org)

The Metropolitan
Museum,
New York
(www.metmuseum.org)

Museum of Fine Arts,
Houston, Texas
(www.mfah.org)

Museum of Fine Arts,
Boston, Massachusetts
(www.mfa.org)

Museum of Modern Art,
New York
(www.moma.org)

The National Gallery
of Art,
Washington D.C.
(www.nga.gov)

Norton Simon Museum,
Pasadena, California
(www.nortonsimon.org)

Allen Memorial
Art Museum,
Oberlin, Ohio
(www.oberlin.edu)

Arkansas Art Centre,
Little Rock, Arkansas
(www.arkarts.com)

Brooklyn Museum,
Brooklyn, New York
(www.brooklynmuseum.org)

Cleveland Museum of Art,
Cleveland, Ohio
(www.clevelandart.org)

Columbus Museum of Art,
Columbus, Ohio
(www.columbusmuseum.org)

Dallas Museum of Art,
Dallas, Texas
(www.dallasmuseumofart.org)

The Hyde Collection,
Glens Falls, New York
(www.hydecollection.org)

Indianapolis Museum
of Art,
Indianapolis, Indiana
(www.imamuseum.org)

Kimbell Art Museum,
Fort Worth, Texas
(www.kimbellart.org)

Meadows Museum at
Southern Methodist
University,
Dallas, Texas
(smu.edu/meadowsmuseum)

Minneapolis Institute
of Art,
Minneapolis, Minnesota
(www.artsmia.org)

Modern Art Museum
of Fort Worth,
Fort Worth, Texas
(themodern.org)

Philadelphia Museum
of Art,
Philadelphia, Pennsylvania
(www.philamuseum.org)

Pierpoint Morgan Library,
New York City, New York
(www.themorgan.org)

Polk Museum of Fine Art,
Lakeland, Florida
(www.polkmuseumofart.org)

St. Louis Art Museum,
St. Louis, Missouri
(stlouis.art.museum)

Smith College Museum
of Art,
Northampton,
Massachusetts
(www.smith.edu)

The Barnes Foundation,
Philadelphia, Pennsylvania
(www.barnesfoundation.org)

Worcester Art Museum,
Worcester, Massachusetts
(www.worcesterart.org)

Yale University Art Gallery,
New Haven, Connecticut
(artgallery.yale.edu)

WHERE TO SEE THIS ARTIST'S WORKS IN THE REST OF THE WORLD

You can see Picasso's works of art in many places around the world, particularly in Europe. It's a good idea to contact the gallery or museum before you visit, to make sure that the work you wish to see is on display.

The State Hermitage Museum,
St. Petersburg, Russia
(www.hermitagemuseum.org)

The Fitzwilliam Museum,
Cambridge, England
(www.fitzmuseum.cam.ac.uk)

Musée National Picasso,
Paris, France
(www.musee-picasso.fr)

Musée National Picasso La Guerre et La Paix,
Vallauris, France
(www.musee-picasso-vallauris.fr)

Museo Picasso Málaga,
Málaga, Spain
(www2.museopicasso malaga.org)

Museu Picasso,
Barcelona, Spain
(www.museupicasso.bcn.es)

National Galleries of Scotland,
Edinburgh, Scotland
(www.nationalgalleries.org)

National Gallery,
London, England
(nationalgallery.org.uk)

Neue Pinakothek,
Munich, Germany
(www.pinakothek.de)

Peggy Guggenheim Museum,
Venice, Italy
(www.guggenheim-venice.it)

Städel Museum,
Frankfurt, Germany
(www.staedelmuseum.de)

Art Gallery of Ontario,
Toronto, Canada
(www.ago.net)

Ashmolean Museum,
Oxford, England
(www.ashmolean.org)

Bilbao Fine Arts Museum,
Bilbao, Spain
(www.museobilbao.com)

Centre Pompidou,
Paris, France
(www.centrepompidou.fr)

The Courtauld Institute of Arts,
London, England
(www.courtauld.ac.uk)

E. G. Bürhle Collection,
Zürich, Switzerland
(www.buehrle.ch)

Haifa Museum,
Haifa, Israel
(hma.org.il/Museum)

Kröller-Müller Museum,
Otterlo, Netherlands
(www.kmm.nl)

Kunstmuseum Basel,
Basel, Switzerland
(www.kunstmuseumbasel.ch)

Ludwig Museum of Contemporary Art,
Budapest, Hungary
(www.ludwigmuseum.hu)

Musée de l'Orangerie,
Paris, France
(www.musee-orangerie.fr)

Musée des Beaux-Arts de Bordeaux,
Bordeaux, France
(www.culture.gouv.fr)

Museum Ludwig,
Cologne, Germany
(www.museenkoeln.de)

National Gallery of Victoria,
Victoria, Australia
(www.ngv.vic.gov.au)

Palazzo Ruspoli,
Rome, Italy
(www.fondazionememmo.com)

Pushkin State Museum of Fine Arts,
Moscow, Russia
(www.museum.ru)

Staatsgalerie,
Stuttgart, Germany
(www.staatsgalerie.de)

Tate Gallery,
London, England
(www.tate.org.uk)

Museo Thyssen-Bornemisza,
Madrid, Spain
(www.museothyssen.org)

Von der Heydt-Museum,
Wuppertal, Germany
(www.von-der-heydt-museum.de)

Wallraf-Richartz-Museum,
Cologne, Germany
(www.museenkoeln.de)

Oskar Reinhart Collection,
Winterthur, Switzerland
(www.roemerholz.ch)

FURTHER READING & WEBSITES

BOOKS

Who was Pablo Picasso?
*True Kelley and
Nancy Harrison,*
Grosset and Dunlap, 2009

Pablo Picasso: Breaking
all the Rules,
True Kelley,
Grosset and Dunlap, 2002

Pablo Picasso
(Artists in their World),
Kate Scarborough,
Franklin Watts, 2002

Pablo Picasso
(Lives of the Artists),
Susie Hodge,
Gareth Stevens Publishing,
2004

Picasso (Masterpieces),
Shelley Swanson Satern,
Franklin Watts, 2004

A Day with Picasso
(Adventures in Art),
Susanne Pfleger,
Prestel, 2000

Painting with Picasso,
*Julie Merberg and
Suzanne Bober,*
Chronicle Books, 2006

Pablo Picasso
(Creative Lives),
Jeremy Wallis,
Heinemann Library, 2001

What makes a
Picasso a Picasso?
Richard Mühlberger,
Viking Children's
Books, 1994

Picasso (Famous Artists),
Anthony Mason,
Franklin Watts, 2001

A Weekend with Picasso,
Florian Rodari,
Rizzoli International
Publications, 1996

A Century of Art,
Claire Tinker,
Belair Publications Ltd,
2006

Cubism (Eye on Art),
Cynthia J. Mines,
Lucent Books, 2006

Cave Paintings to Picasso:
the inside Scoop on 50
Famous Masterpieces,
Henry M. Sayer,
Chronicle Books, 2003

WEBSITES

www.pablopicasso.org

www.picasso.fr

pablo-
picasso.paintings.name

www.ibiblio.org/wm/paint/
tl/20th/cubism.html

www.guggenheimcollectio
n.org/site/artist_bio_126.ht
ml

www.mykidsart.com.au/Pa
blo_Picasso_Famous_Artist
s_My_Kids_Art.html

www.thekidswindow.co.uk
/News/Pablo_Picasso.htm

www.guggenheimcollectio
n.org/site/artist_works_126
_0.html

www.alifetimeofcolor.com/
study/g_cubism.html

www.robinurton.com/histo
ry/cubism.htm

www.guggenheimcollectio
n.org/site/movement_
works_Cubism_0.html

www.ibiblio.org/wm/paint/
glo/cubism

www.theartgallery.com.au/
kidsart/learn/cubism

www.artic.edu/artaccess/
AA_Modern/pages/
MOD_1.shtml

www.bbc.co.uk/history/
historic_figures/picasso_
pablo.shtml

www.moma.org/explore/
multimedia/audios/1/6

GLOSSARY

Collage—From the French verb *coller*, meaning "to glue," collages are images made from all sorts of materials, glued to the surface. The technique was first introduced by Picasso and Braque in about 1912

Cubism—The movement started by Picasso and Braque in which artists represented their subjects from several angles at once, rather than from just one point of view

Draughtsman—Someone who is skilful at drawing

Exposition Universelle—World Fairs were large public exhibitions where all countries could exhibit and the host country could show off its achievements. The Exposition Universelle was the name of most of the Parisian World Fairs (there were eight in Paris, from 1855 to 1937)

Futurism—An art movement founded in 1909, comprising mainly Italian artists, which rejected everything from the past in favor of modernism. Futurists loved machinery and movement

Impasto—An Italian word which describes the thickness of paint on the surface of a painting. Impasto paint is applied so thickly that it stands proud of the surface and brush marks can be seen clearly

Mural—Any kind of wall painting, but it is not the same as fresco which describes a particular method of painting on plaster.

Objet Trouvés—This means literally "found objects" and is mostly associated with the Surrealist movement. It refers to everyday practical objects which might be found anywhere and are given new meaning by the artist, like Picasso's bicycle saddle and handlebars becoming a bull's head

Representation—Until the introduction of abstract art in the 20th century, all Western art "represented" or depicted people, objects and scenes in a recognizable way. Visual "rules" about how things were represented began with the 14th century artist Giotto and artists of the Renaissance.

Surrealism—The word "surrealism," first coined by Picasso's friend Apollinaire in 1917, was used to describe art which included strange, dream-like imagery and odd combinations

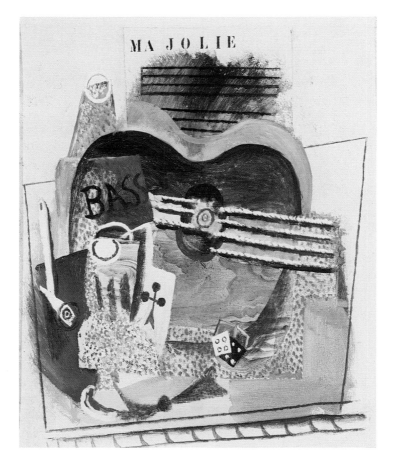

INDEX

ACKNOWLEDGMENTS

Picture Credits t=top, b=bottom, c=center, l=left, r=right, OFC=outside front cover.

All works by Pablo Picasso © Succession Picasso/DACS 1997.

AKG/Sotheby's. Photo © AKG London; 32tl. Photograph of Picasso, 1933, Man Ray © Man Ray Trust/ADAGP, Paris and DACS, London 1997 (Photo © AKG London); 28tl. Photo © AKG London; 6bl, 7bl, 7c, 8bl, OFCb & 10/11cb, 12tl, 12cb, 14cb, 16tl, 27tl, 28tl, 31tl. Photo © AKG London/AP; 25tr, 24/25c. Photo © AKG London/Paul Almasy; 31br. Photo © AKG London/David Douglas Duncan; 16c, 16br. John Daniels/Ardea London; 33b. Mary Evans Picture Library; 6tl, OFCt & 7tr, 26bl. FORBES Magazine Collection, New York/Bridgeman Art Library, London; 7br. Galerie Jan Krugier, Geneva. Photo © AKG London; 33t. Design Council; 34bl. First published by The Independent (Jason Bennetto, Crime Correspondent); 35tr. Pablo Picasso, Les Demoiselles d'Avignon. Paris (June-July 1907) oil on canvas, 8' x 7'8" (243.9 x 233.7cm). The Museum of Modern Art, New York. Acquired through the Lillie P. Bliss Bequest. Photograph © 1997 The Museum of Modern Art, New York; 20/21c & detail 20cb. Museum of Art, Philadelphia. Photo © AKG London; 21tr, 29br. Museum of Modern Art, New York. Photo © AKG London/Erich Lessing; 10bl. Museo Nacional Reina Sofia, Madrid. Photo © AKG London; 26/27c & 27bl. Musee Picasso, Barcelona. Photo © AKG London; 9cr. Musee Picasso, Paris. Photo © AKG London; 15br, 9tl, 13bl, 17tl, 25br. Family of Saltimbanques, Chester Dale Collection © 1997 Board of Trustees, National Gallery of Art, Washington, 1905, canvas, 2.128 x 2.296 (83¾ x 90⅜); framed: 2.404 x 2.563 (94⅝ x 100⅞); 18tl & detail 18bl, 18br & 19tl.19tl. National Gallery of Art, Washington. Photo © AKG London; 19tr. Les Acrobats, 1930, Fernand Leger © ADAGP, Paris and DACS, London 1997 (Private Collection. Photo © AKG London); 11tr & 11br, OFC (main image) & 15tr, 22tl, 35bl. Pinacoteca di Brera, Milan. Photo © AKG London; 28bl. Pushkin Museum, Moscow. Photo © AKG London/Erich Lessing; 19cb, 22/23b. Sammlung Heinz Berggruen, Geneva. Photo © AKG London; OFCc &13tr. Totenmahl, Renato Guttuso © DACS 1997 (Sammlung Ludwig, Aachen. Photo © AKG London); 30tl & 34t. Solomon R. Guggenheim Museum, New York. Photo © AKG London; 9bl. Staatl. Russisches Museum, St. Petersburg. Photo © AKG London; 31tr. Music, 1910, Henri Matisse © Succession H Matisse/DACS 1997 (State Hermitage, St. Petersburg. Photo © AKG London); 10tr. State Hermitage, St. Petersburg. Photo © AKG London/Erich Lessing; 23tr. © Photo RMN-Arnaudet (Musee Picasso, Paris); 32bl. © Photo RMN (Musee Picasso, Paris); 14tr. Tate Gallery, London. Photo © AKG London/Erich Lessing; 28/29c. Dr. Werner Muensterberger Collection, London/Bridgeman Art Library, London; 20tl.

NOTE TO READERS